D. S. Publishers (India)
the Bookmaster
DELHI

Language Skills

Pre-Primary Learning Skills
B

Letters & Words

Shab

This book belongs to

____

____

AF798540

D. S. Publishers (India)

First Published 2001
22nd Reprint 2022

ISBN 978-81-8023-016-5

Published by
DS Publishers (India)
7/7 Ansari Road, Daryaganj
New Delhi 110 002
+91 11 4156 3757
info@dspublishers.com
www.dspublishers.com

Type-setting and Cover Design by
Lovika Arts

Printed at
Balaji Offset

135

PREFACE

Children of the ages between 3 years and 5 years are at the Pre-Primary stage of learning, and just about awakened to their sensory skills.

This series of books is basically revolving round children of these ages — and are thus directed towards the development of the skills to which the tiny beings are getting introduced to. They are being initiated into the concepts that are necessary for further progress of the learning procedures.

This set of books deals separately with specific language skills. With these books at hand, followed by the guidance of the teacher or parents will take the children ahead in fixing in their minds the correct concepts necessary for further education.

The activities enshrined in these books help the child in developing his/her basic skills of reading and writing.

Trace the letters.

A	 APPLE	A	A	A
B	 BOY	B	B	B
C	CAKE 	C	C	C
D	 DOG	D	D	D
E	 ELEPHANT	E	E	E
F	 FAN	F	F	F

Teacher/Parents : Tell the children the sound of letters. Talk through the shapes of letters.

G	 GRAPES	G	G	G
H	 HEN	H	H	H
I	INKPOT 	I	I	I
J	 JUG	J	J	J
K	 KING	K	K	K
L	LION 	L	L	L
M	 MONKEY	M	M	M

N	 NEST	N	N	N
O	 OWL	O	O	O
P	PEAR 	P	P	P
Q	QUEEN 	Q	Q	Q
R	 RABBIT	R	R	R
S	SHIP 	S	S	S
T	 TREE	T	T	T

U	 UMBRELLA	U	U	U
V	 VAN	V	V	V
W	 WATCH	W	W	W
X	 XYLOPHONE	X	X	X
Y	YACHT 	Y	Y	Y
Z	ZEBRA 	Z	Z	Z

Match the letters.

B	E
D	D
E	M
F	B
N	F
M	N

Teacher/Parents : Help the children to identify the letters.

Q

S

P

U

W

T

X

P

T

W

X

Q

S

U

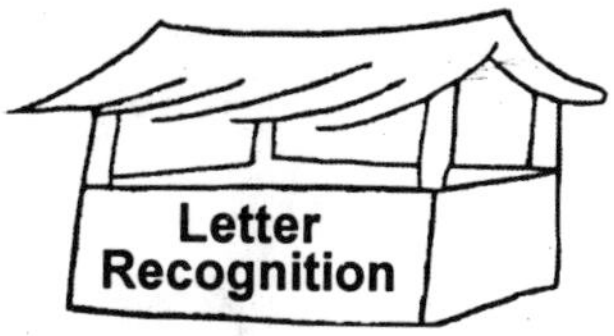

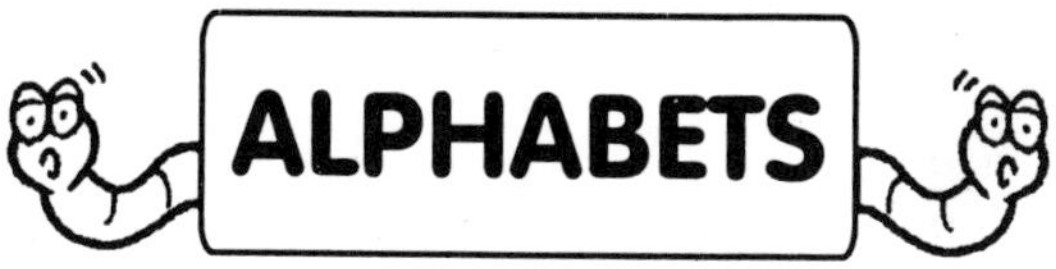

Capital and small letters

Trace the small letters.

A	a	a	a	a
B	b	b	b	b
C	c	c	c	c
D	d	d	d	d
E	e	e	e	e
F	f	f	f	f

Teacher/Parents

Ask the child to read and identify the letters. Talk through the shapes of small letters.

G	g	g	g	g
H	h	h	h	h
I	i	i	i	i
J	j	j	j	j
K	k	k	k	k
L	l	l	l	l
M	m	m	m	m

N	n	n	n	n
O	o	o	o	o
P	p	p	p	p
Q	q	q	q	q
R	r	r	r	r
S	s	s	s	s
T	t	t	t	t

U	u	u	u	u
V	v	v	v	v
W	w	w	w	w
X	x	x	x	x
Y	y	y	y	y
Z	z	z	z	z

SAME AND DIFFERENT

Look at the pictures carefully. Circle the two pictures that are exactly the same.

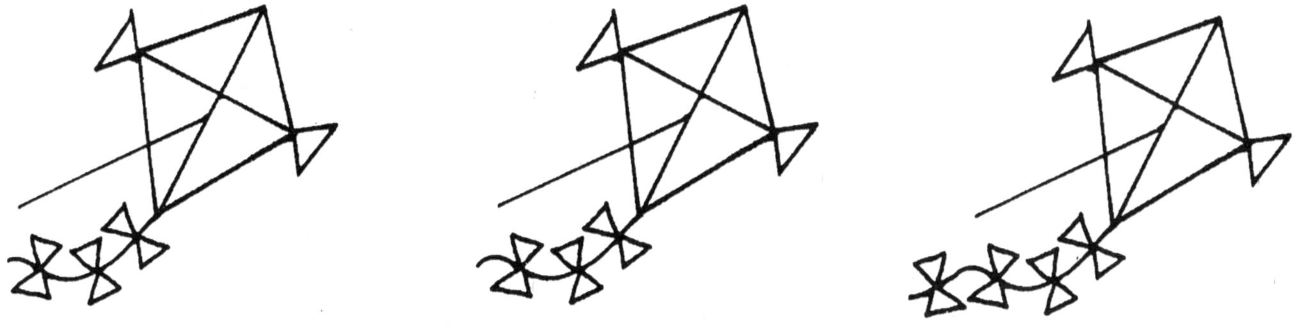

eacher/Parents How is the pair of pictures similar? How is the other different?

LOOK ALIKE

Cross the odd one out.

b	b	b	d	b
j	j	i	j	j
m	m	m	m	n
p	q	p	p	p
e	e	c	e	e
r	r	r	t	r

u u u u n

q g q q q

h h h n h

w w v w w

d d d a d

i i i i l

y z y y y

Visual Discrimination

LOOK ALIKE

Small letters

Circle the letters that are the same.

i	j	j	l	t
p	b	q	q	g
u	n	m	n	h
f	r	f	t	l
a	d	p	c	a
x	u	v	v	w
p	q	b	d	b

Circle the letters that are the same.

M	W	N	W	V
O	Q	P	Q	D
Y	Z	X	Y	U
C	P	P	S	G
J	L	I	T	J
V	U	V	Y	W
H	E	F	F	Z

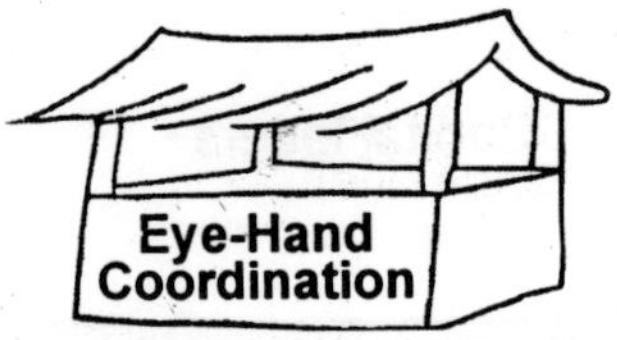

ALPHABETS

Small and capital letters

Let us write capital 'A'.

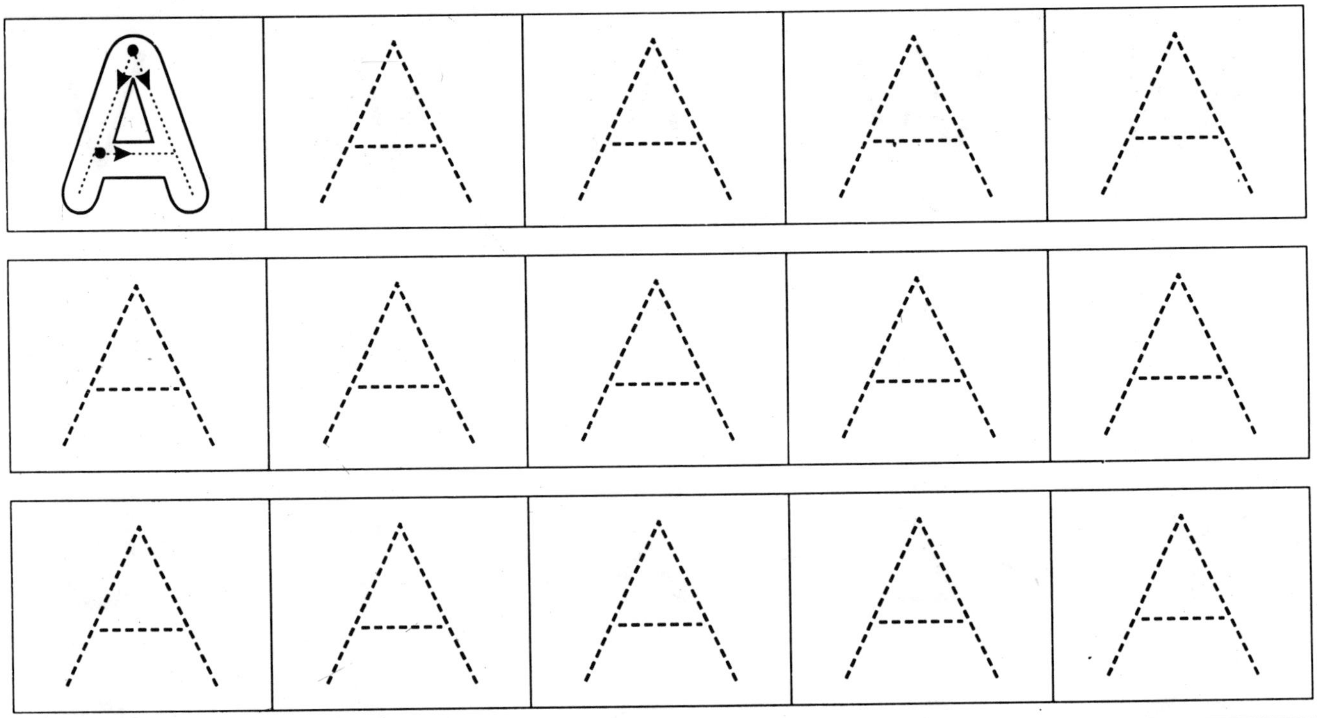

Let us write small 'a'.

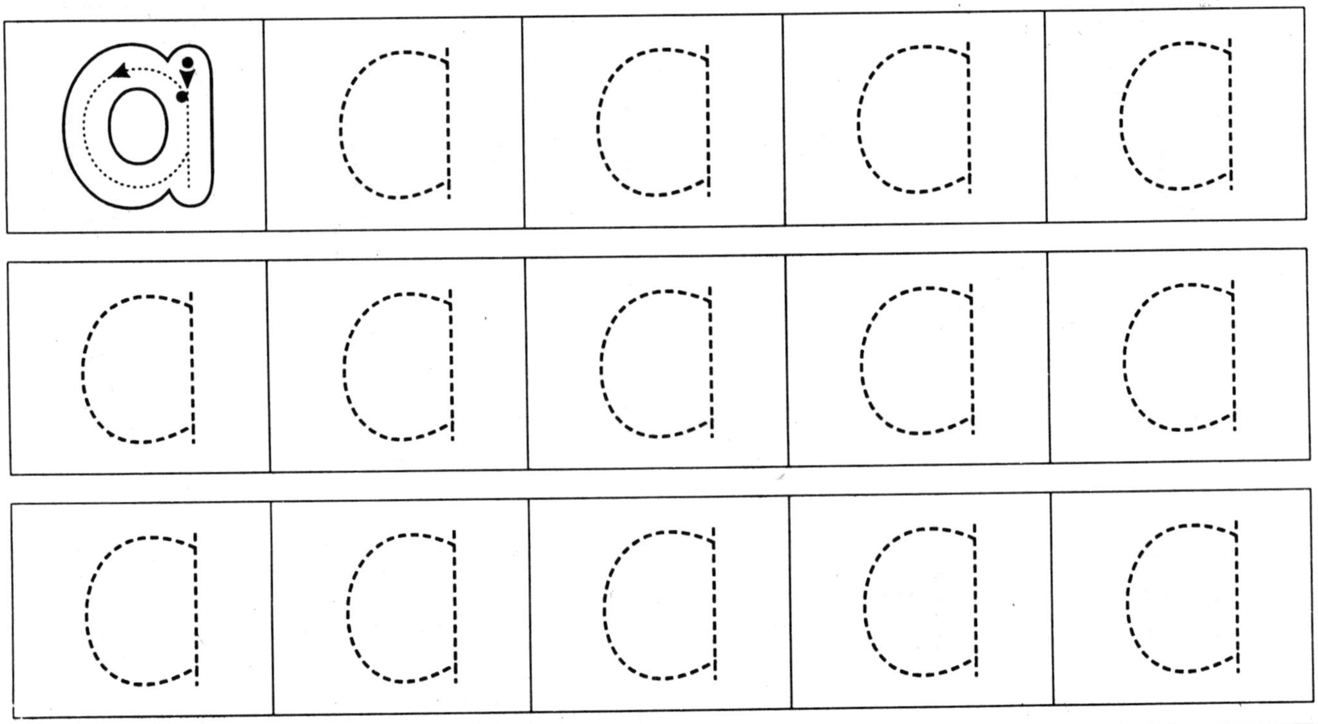

Teacher/Parents : Direct the children in tracing the capital and small letters.

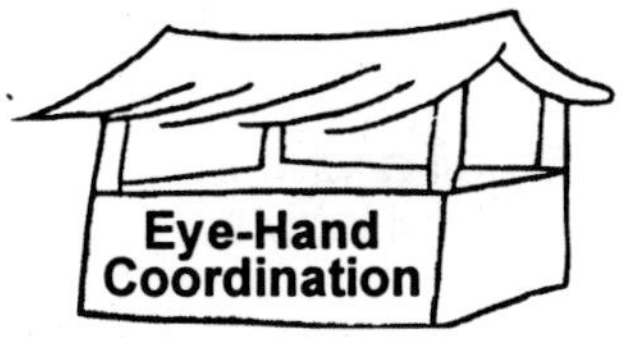

Small and capital letters

Let us write capital 'B'.

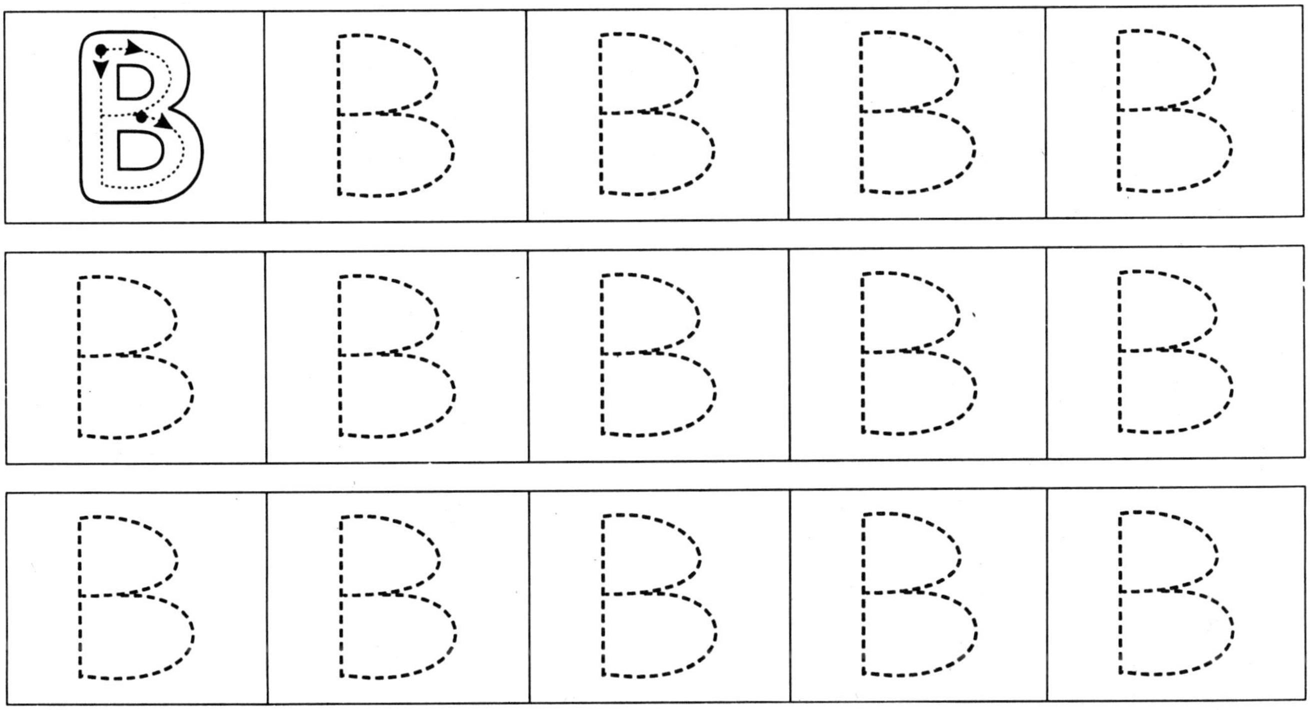

Let us write small 'b'.

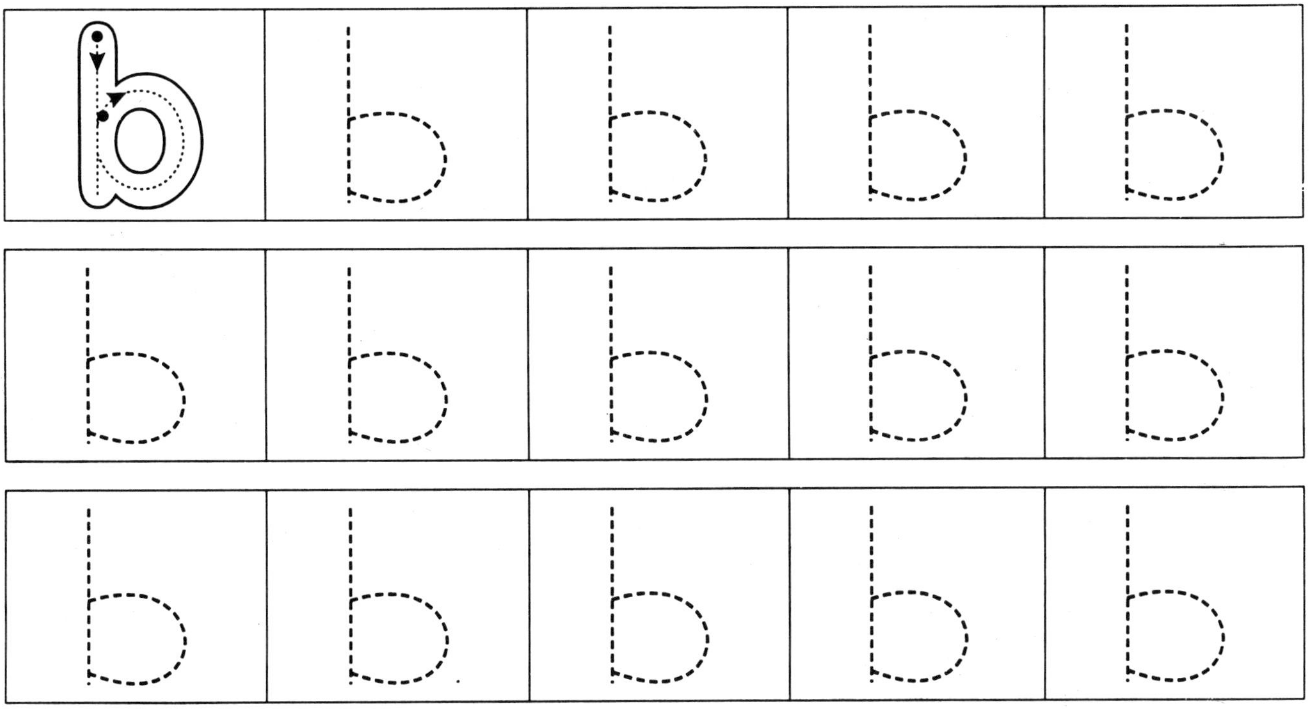

Trace the letters.

C	c	C	c
D	d	D	d
E	e	E	e
F	f	F	f
G	g	G	g
H	h	H	h

I	i	I	i
J	j	J	j
K	k	K	k
L	l	L	l
M	m	M	m
N	n	N	n

O o O o

P p P p

Q q Q q

R r R r

S s S s

T t T t

U u U u

V v V v

W w W w

X x X x

Y y Y y

Z z Z z

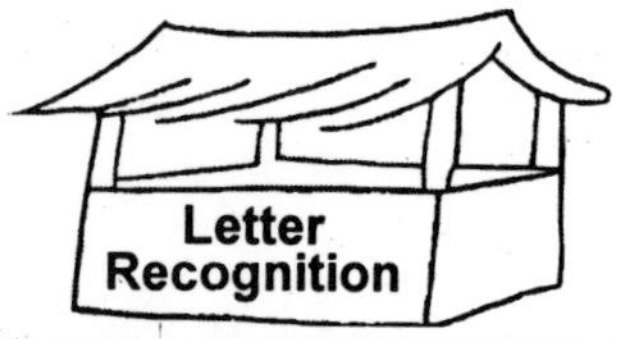

ALPHABETS

Match

Match the capital letter with the small one.

B •	• f
N •	• z
F •	• l
U •	• n
Z •	• b
L •	• u

V •	• d
A •	• j
J •	• v
Q •	• r
D •	• a
R •	• q

Teacher/Parents : Help the children to make out the difference in the shapes of capital and small letters.

Match the letters.

O •	• s
M •	• i
W •	• p
I •	• e
E •	• o
S •	• w
P •	• m

T Y C K H G X

g x t c y k h

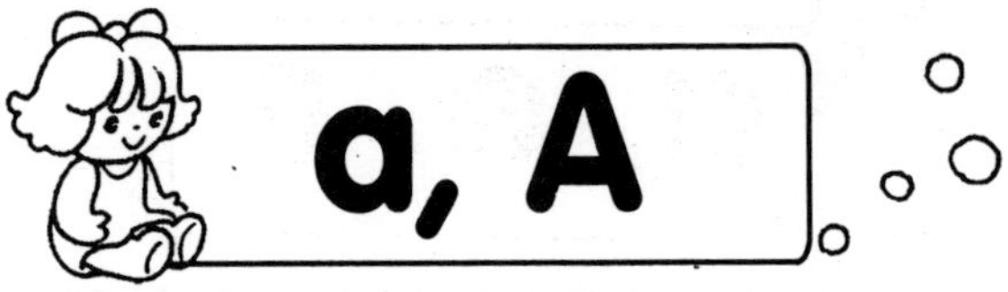

Recognise

Colour all the apples with capital A red.
Colour all the apples with small a green.

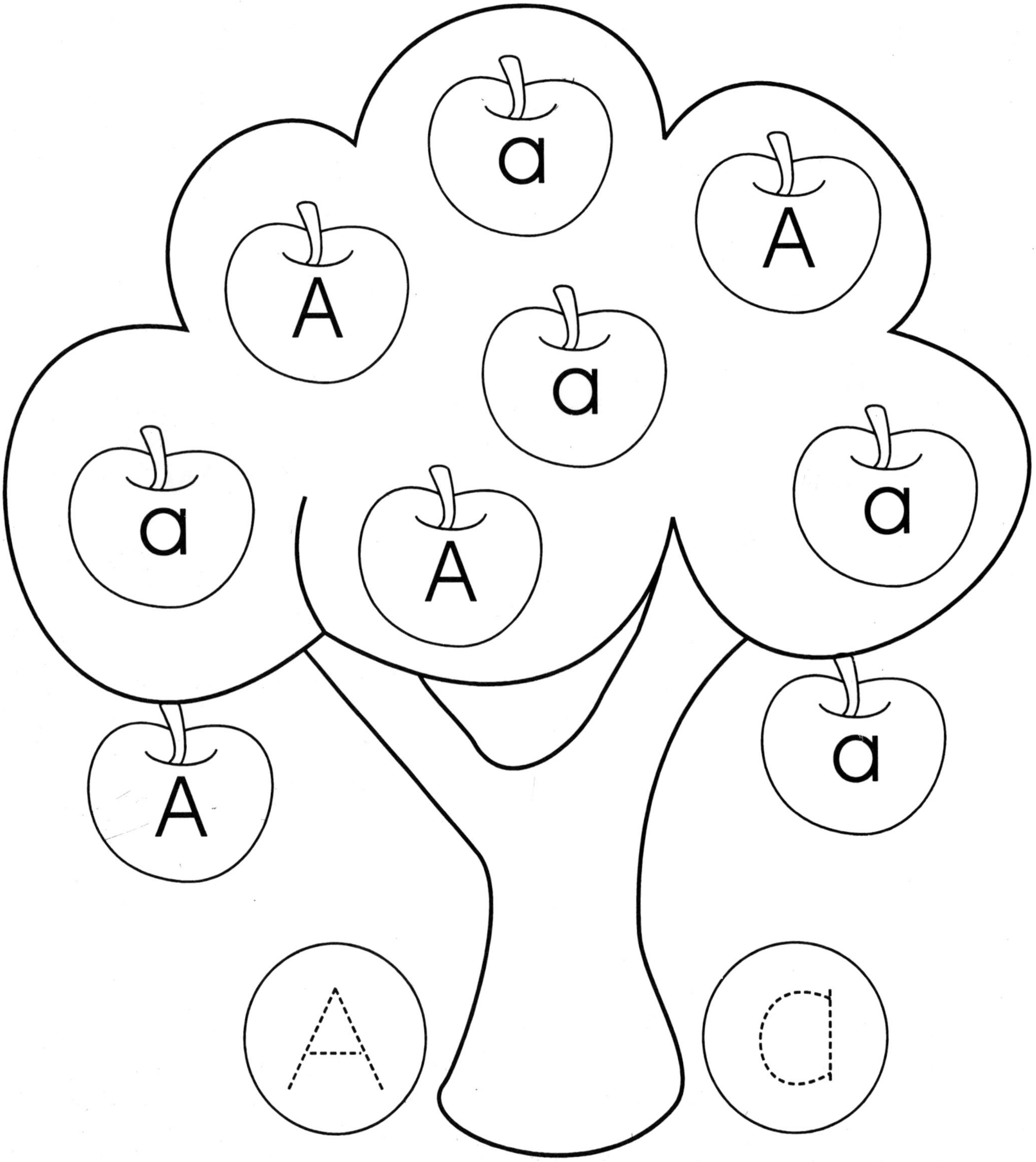

Teacher/Parents : Ask the child to count the capital letters and the number of small letters separately.

a, e, o

Letter-Sound Discrimination

Recognise beginning letter-sounds of a, e, and o.

Circle the picture that does not have the same beginning sound as the first picture.

 apple			
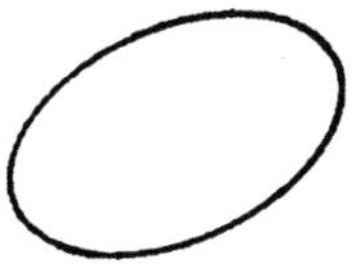 egg			
 owl		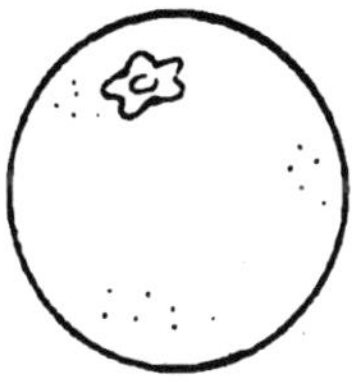	

Trace the words.

apple apple apple

egg egg egg egg

owl owl owl owl

Teacher/Parents : Name the pictures. Help the children to know that the sound of a, e, and o is different from each other.

Visual Discrimination

a, e, o

Differentiate beginning letter-sounds of a, e, and o.

Name the pictures. Circle the letters a, e and o in the words.

b a l l

d o l l

h o r s e

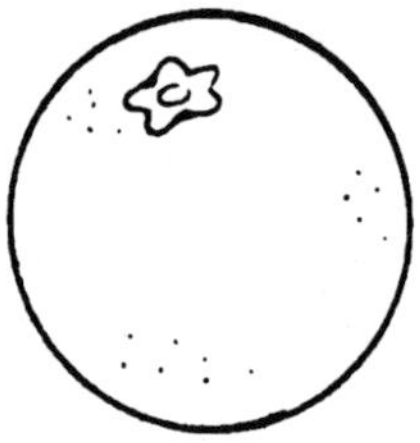

o r a n g e

c a t

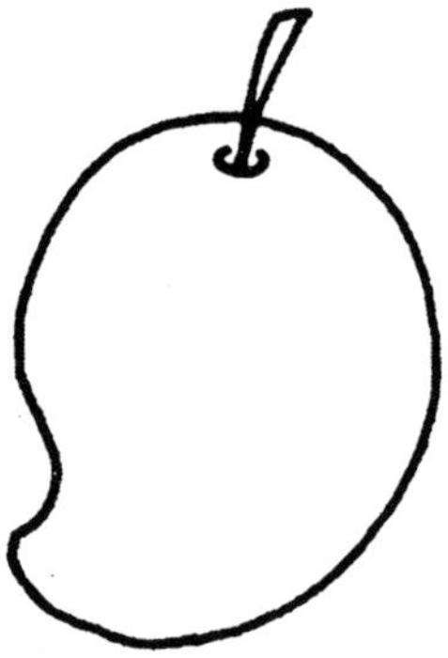

m a n g o

Teacher/Parents : Ask the child to name the picture. Help him to differentiate a, e or o in each word from the other letters.

b, d, p

Look at the picture carefully. Say the word aloud. Then fill in the first letter.

_ o y

_ u c k

_ a t

_ e a r

Teacher/Parents

Name the picture. Help the child to write first letter of the word with the help of beginning letter - sound of the name.

b, d, p

Cross out the word that is not the same as others in each row.

1.	bear	bear	pear	bear
2.	dress	dress	dress	press
3.	pot	dot	pot	pot
4.	door	door	poor	door
5.	boat	boat	goat	boat
6.	pear	pear	pear	dear
7.	big	pig	big	big
8.	bad	bad	dad	bad
9.	cool	fool	cool	cool

Teacher/Parents : Read the words to the child. Let the child note the difference of beginning letter-sound in the word which is not alike.

b, d, p

Colour the pictures that begin with the same sound as the first picture in each row. Cross the odd one out.

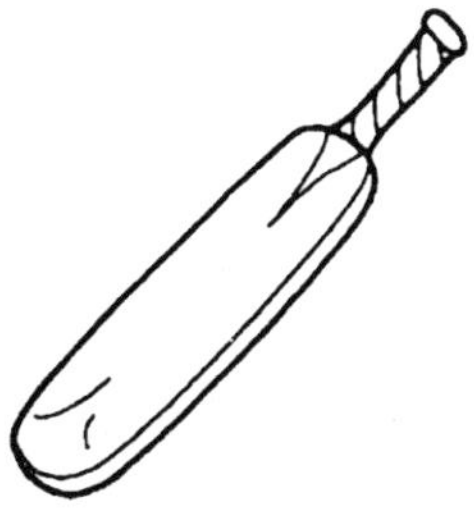

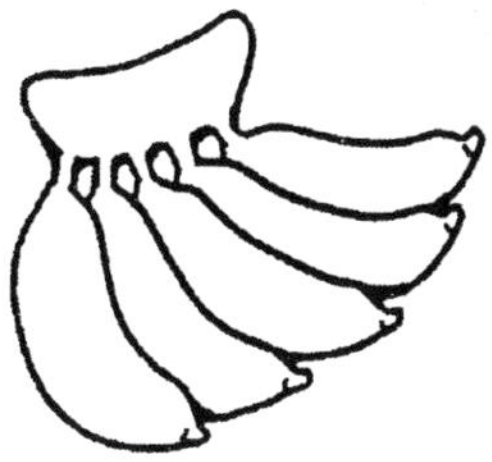

Teacher/Parents : Ask the child to recognise the beginning letter-sound of the picture. Help him to give the suitable colour to the picture.

c, g

Circle the pictures that begin with c as in cat.

Circle the pictures that begin with g as in girl.

Teacher/Parents : Help the children to recognise and then name the pictures. Stress the beginning letter-sound of each word before circling the picture.

Eye-Hand Co-ordination

c, g

Write the words beginning with c and g.

Trace and write the words.

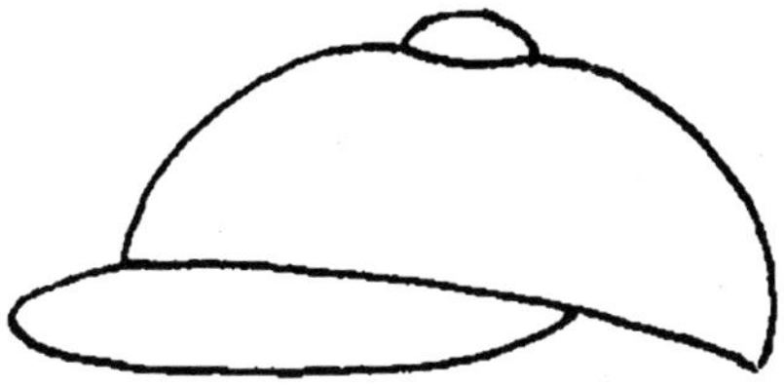

cap ______________________

coat ______________________

cow ______________________

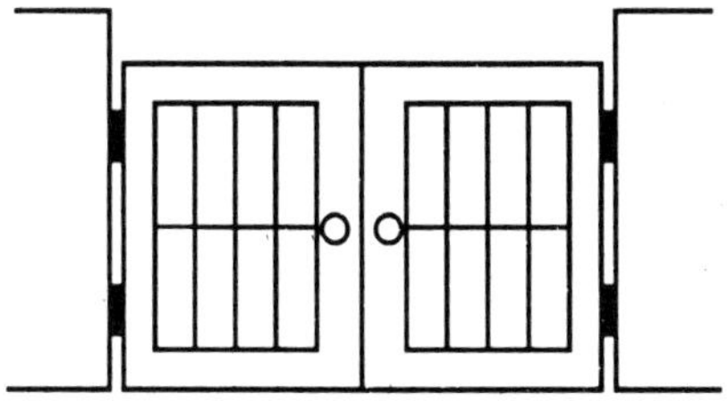

gate ______________________

goat ______________________

Teacher/Parents : Read the words to the child. Encourage him to identify the letter c or g in each word.

c, g

Write the correct word in the space given.

clown		_ _ _
cloud		_ _ _ _ _ _
candle		_ _ _ _ _
cock		_ _ _ _ _ _
carrot		_ _ _ _
car		_ _ _ _
cook		_ _ _ _ _

c, g

Draw lines to join the words to the correct pictures.

girl

giraffe

goat

grasshopper

goose

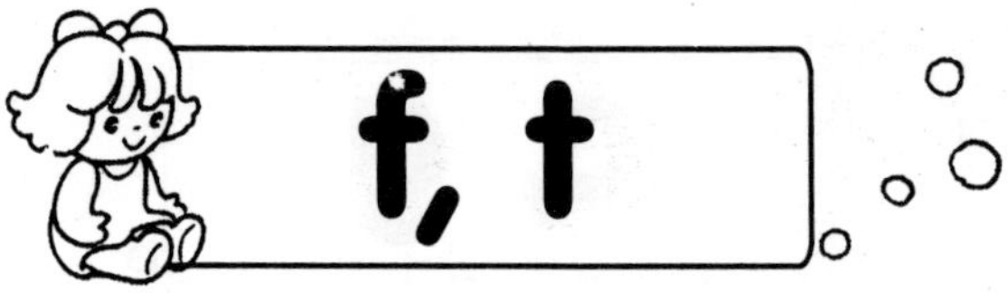

Name the pictures. Colour the pictures that begin with the same letter f as in foot.

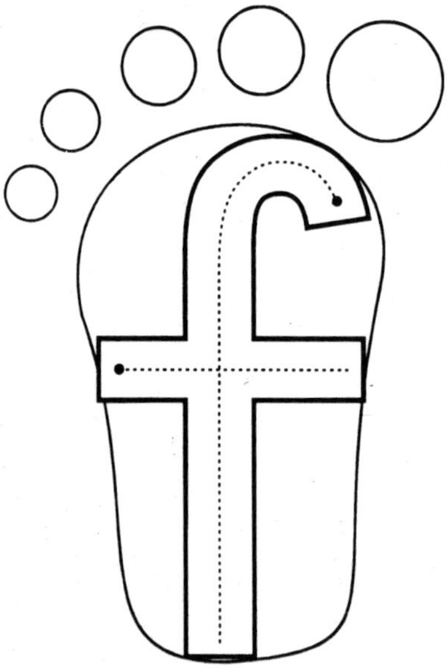

Name the pictures. Colour the pictures that begin with the same letter t as in telephone.

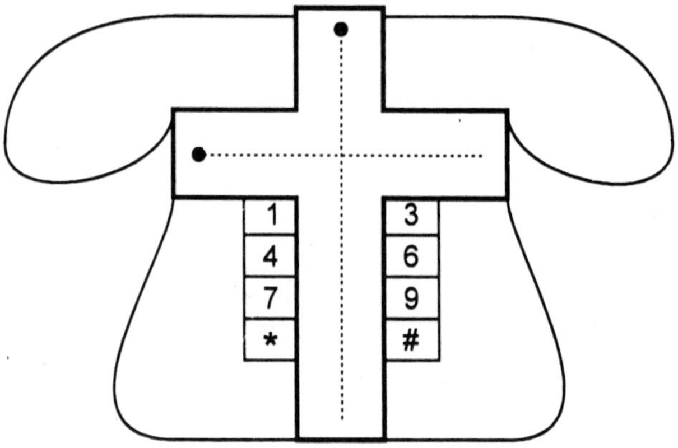

Teacher/Parents : 'Talk through' the shapes of the letters 'f' (round and down, then across) and 't' (down the telephone and across the hand set). Name the pictures. Ask the children to recognise the first letter-sound of the words.

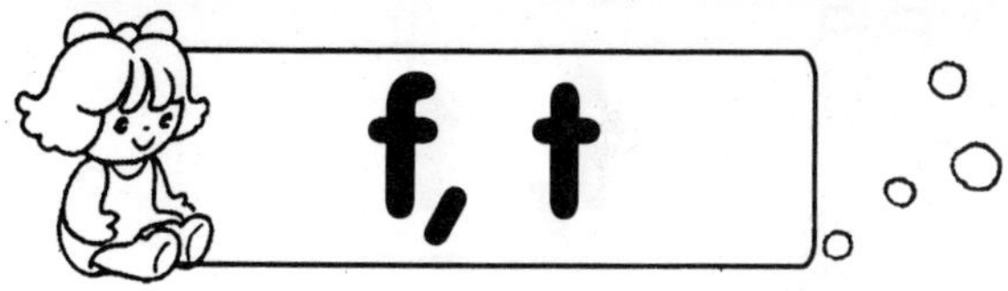

Pick out the correct word from the box and write next to the each picture.

ten
teeth
train
toe
tiger
towel

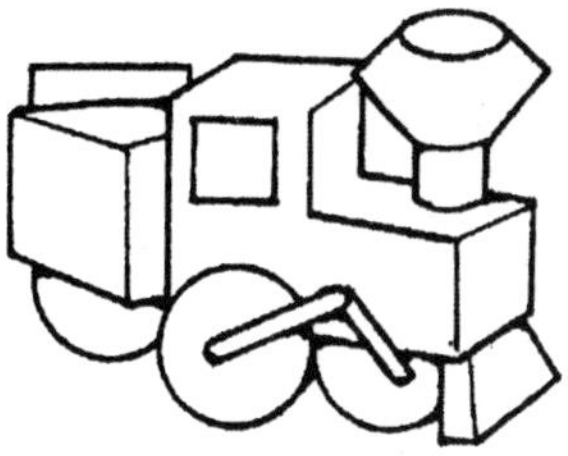 _ _ _ _ _

 _ _ _ _ _

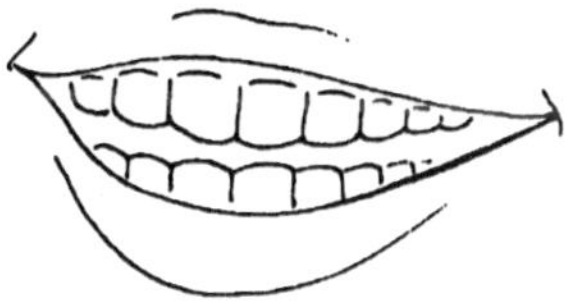 _ _ _ _ _

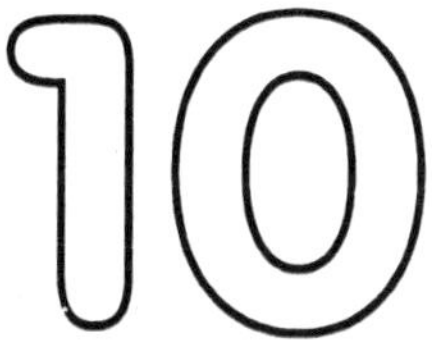 _ _ _ _ _

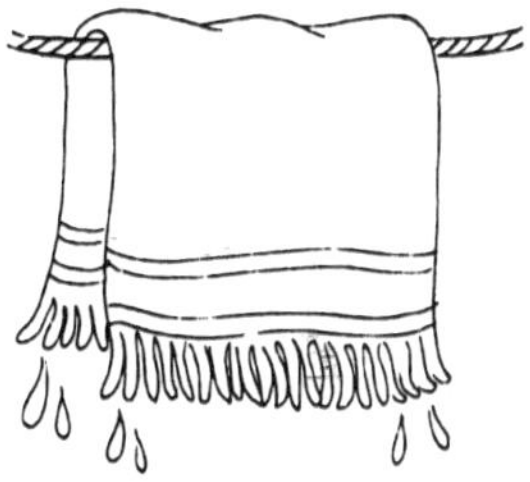 _ _ _ _ _

 _ _ _ _ _

f, t

Colour the pictures. Trace and write the words.

five fat frogs

three tiny turtles

m, n

Tony has a <u>mug</u> of <u>milk</u> with the letter <u>m</u>.
Colour all the <u>mugs</u> that have the same letter <u>m</u>.

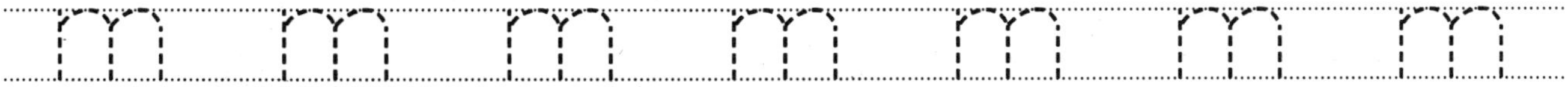

Mona has a <u>notebook</u> with the letter <u>n</u>.
Colour all the <u>notebooks</u> that have the letter <u>n</u>.

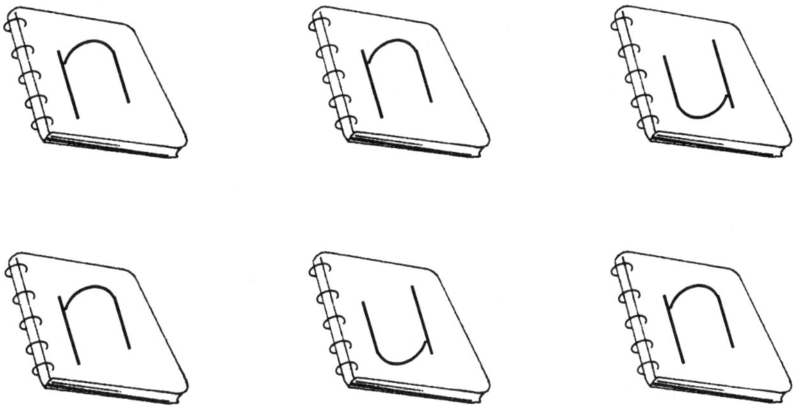

Teacher/Parents : Young children have confusion in letters m, n, u and w. Ask them to trace the letters and note the difference.

m, n

Trace the letters m and n.

Name the pictures. Complete the words.

monkey

moon

mango

melon

man

woman

Teacher/Parents

Use more words that have letters m and n.

i, j, l

Recognise beginning letter-sound of i, j and l.

Name the pictures. Draw lines to join the pictures that have the same beginning sound.

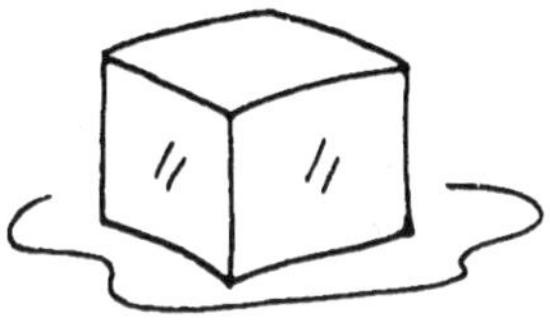

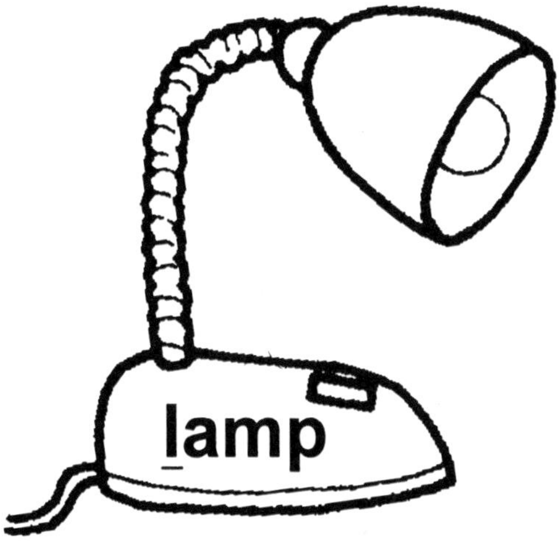

Teacher/Parents : Name the pictures to the child. Stress on the beginning sounds of i, j and l of the words.

i, j, l

Trace and write words beginning with i, j, and l.

Trace and write the words.

ink ink

ice ice

jug jug

jam jam

lamp lamp

lion lion

Teacher/Parents : Help the child to differentiate the letters i, j, and l by tracing and writing.

i, j, l

Draw lines to join the words to the correct pictures.

lion

ice-cream

ice

lotus

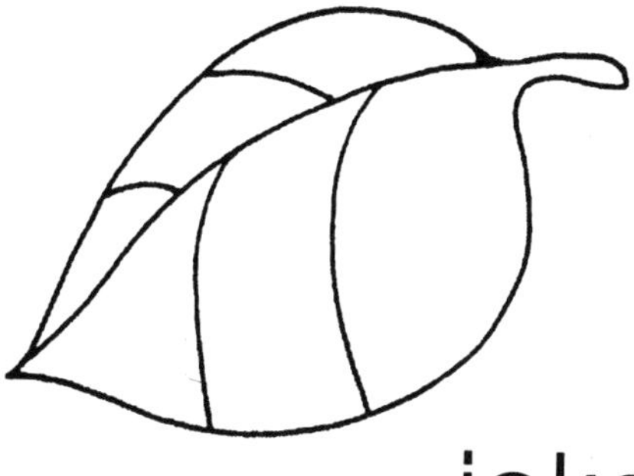

leaf

joker

Letter-Sound Recognition

h, k

Recognise beginning letter-sound of h and k.

Name the pictures. Circle the pictures that begin with h as in hen.

hen

Name the pictures. Circle the pictures that begin with k as in king.

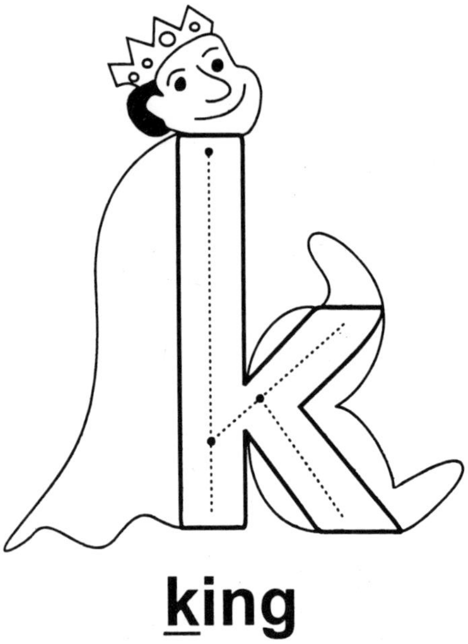

king

Teacher/Parents

Talk through the shapes and sounds of the letters h and k. Name the pictures aloud and help children to recognise the first letter-sound of the words.

h, k

Trace and write letters and words.

Write the letters.

h h h

k k k

Trace and write the words.

key key key

hen hen hen

hat hat hat

kite kite kite

r, s

Recognise beginning letter-sound of r and s.

Circle the pictures beginning with the letter r as in read.

read

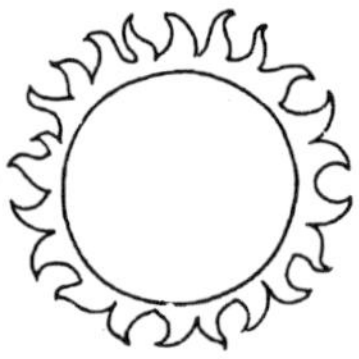

Circle the pictures beginning with the letter s as in sun.

sun

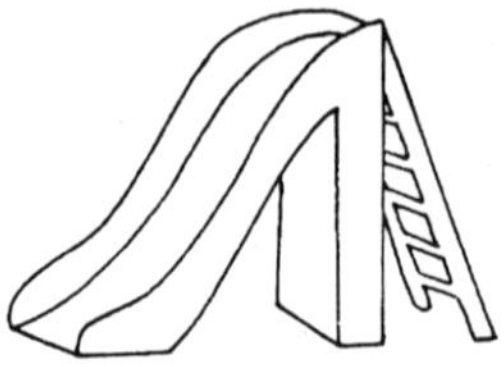

Teacher/Parents : Help the child to know the letter-name followed by the letter-sound.

r, s

Match pictures and words beginning with letter-sound r and s.

Write the correct word under each picture.

sit

run

shoes

socks

robot

radio

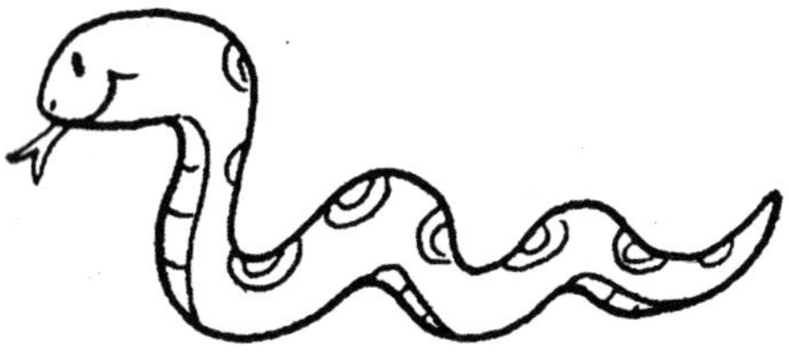

rat

snake

Teacher/Parents Name the pictures to the children. Help them to recognise the words accordingly.

u, v, w

Match the
letter to
the picture.

Name the picture aloud. Draw a line to join the picture to the correct beginning letter.

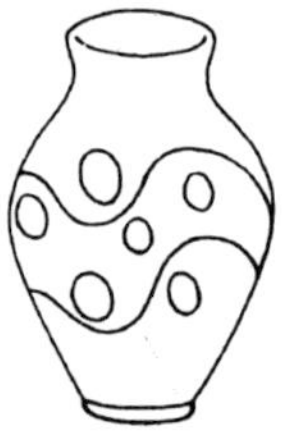

u
v

v
w

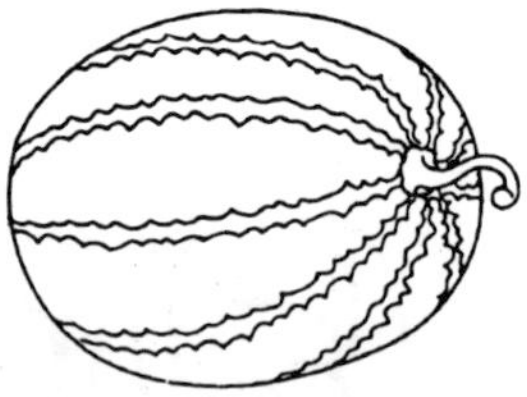

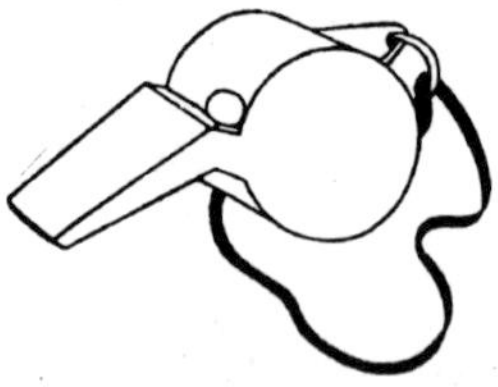

w
u

u
w

u
v

w
v

Teacher/Parents Name the pictures. Stress on the beginning sound of the names of pictures.

Word Recognition

U, V, W

Write words beginning with u, v and w.

Trace and write the words.

umbrella umbrella

van van

watch watch

vase vase

urn urn

x, y, z

Count x, y and z separately. How many x, y and z can you find here.

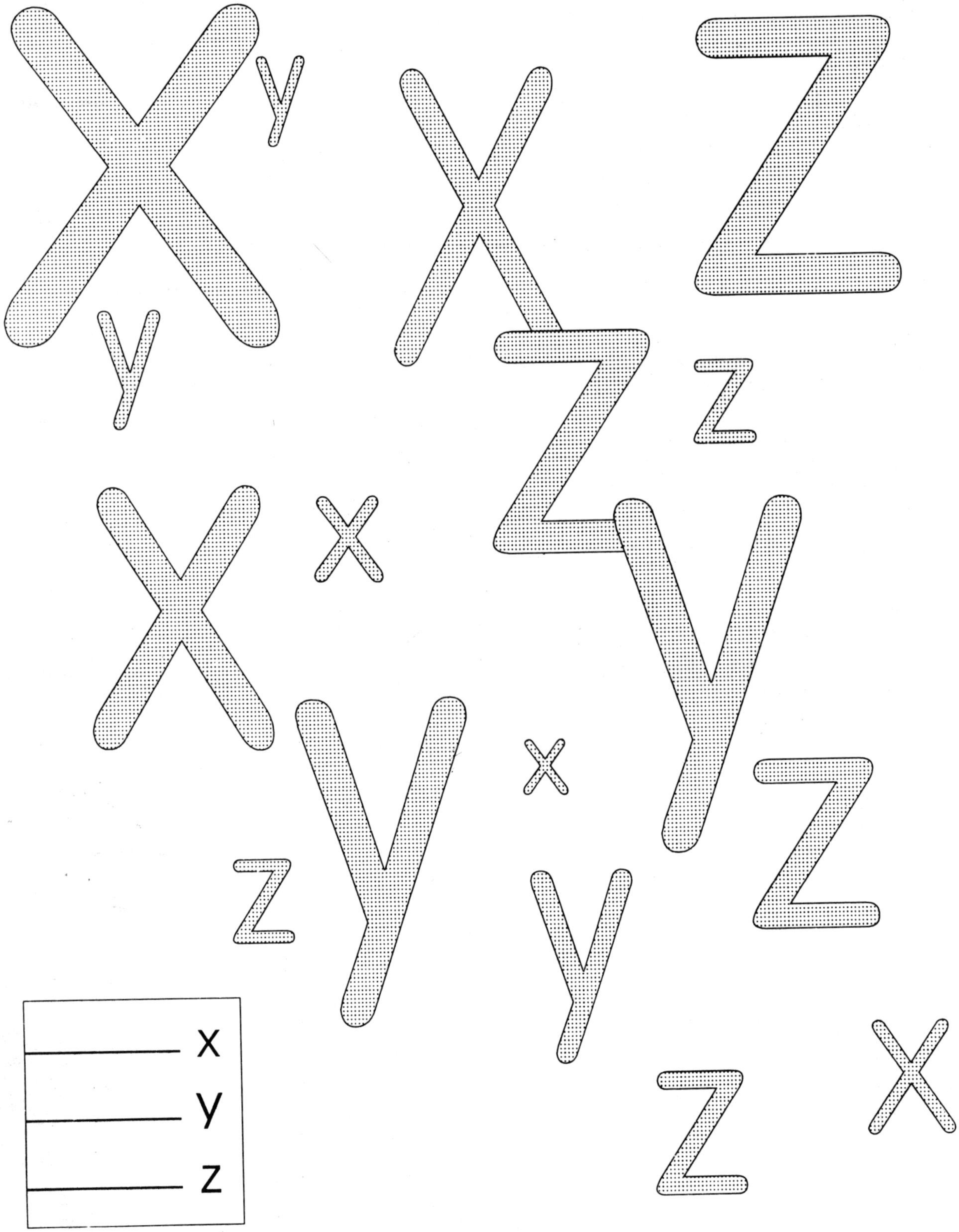

______	x
______	y
______	z

x, y, z

Complete the words. Now match the pictures with the words.

zip

xmas tree

yak

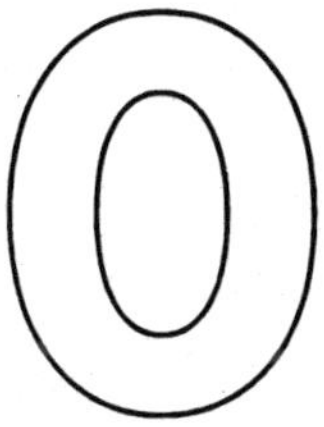

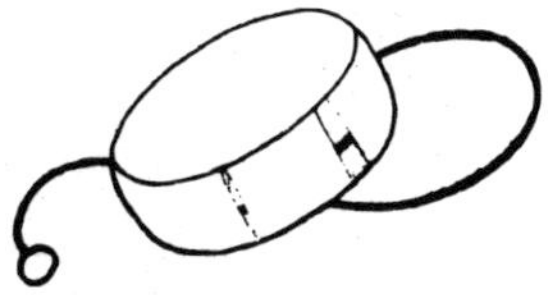

xylophone

yo-yo

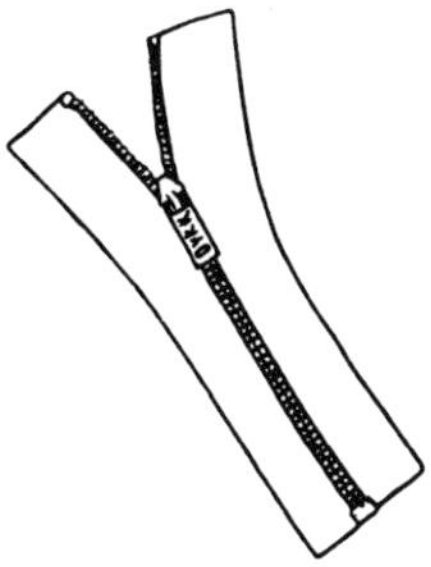

zero

yacht

zebra

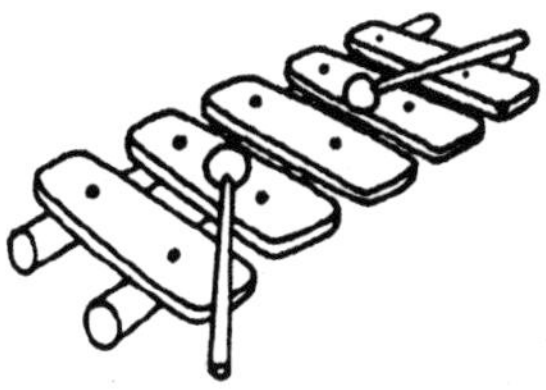

Trace the words.

girl

fish

nest

duck

owl

bird

top

mug

kite

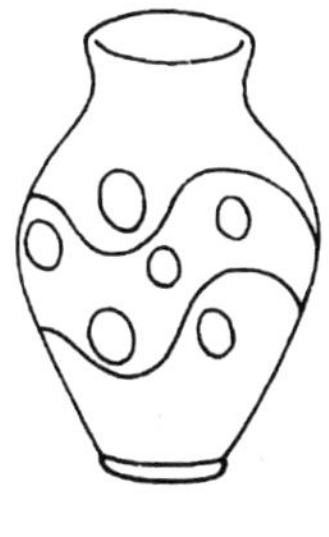

vase

star

Fill in the missing letters.

A ____	B ____	____ c
D ____	____ e	____ f
G ____	____ h	____ i
J ____	K ____	____ l
M ____	____ n	O ____

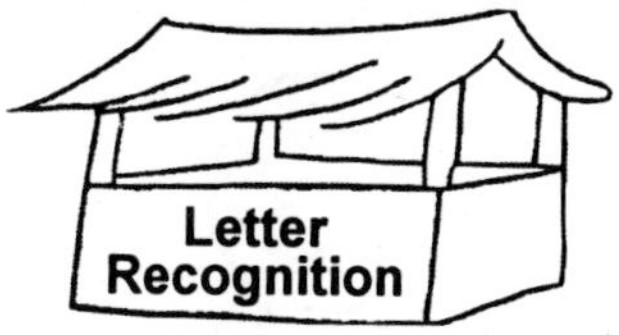

REVISION

Match beginning sound of words with letters.

Name the picture first. Write the beginning letter of the picture on the line given.

____

____

____

____

____

____

____

____

____

____

____

____

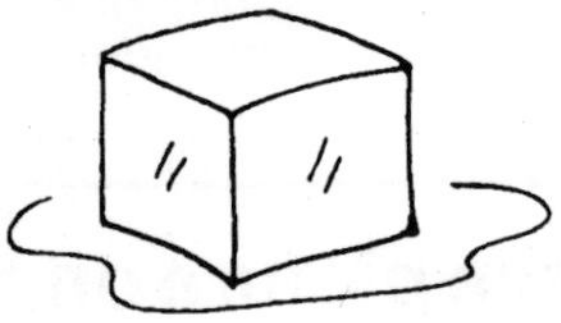

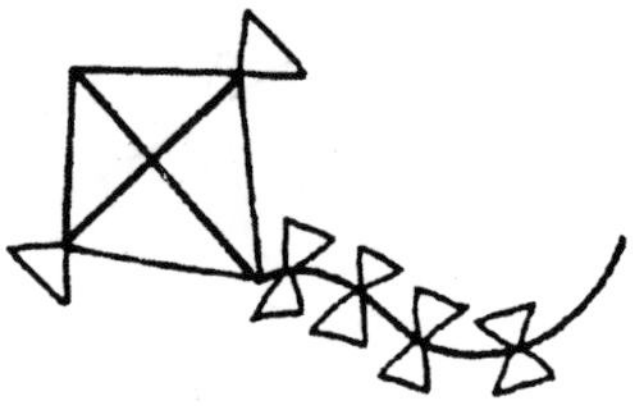
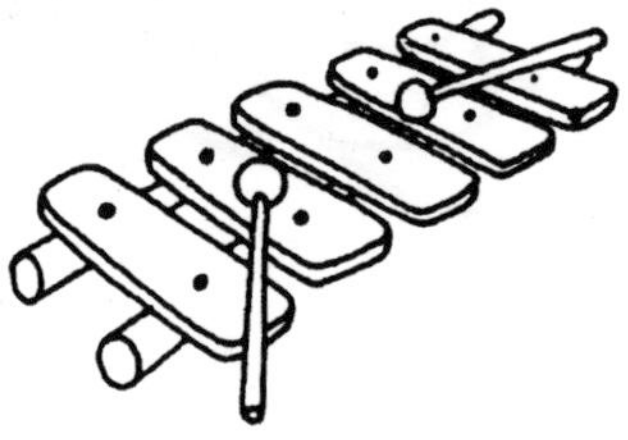

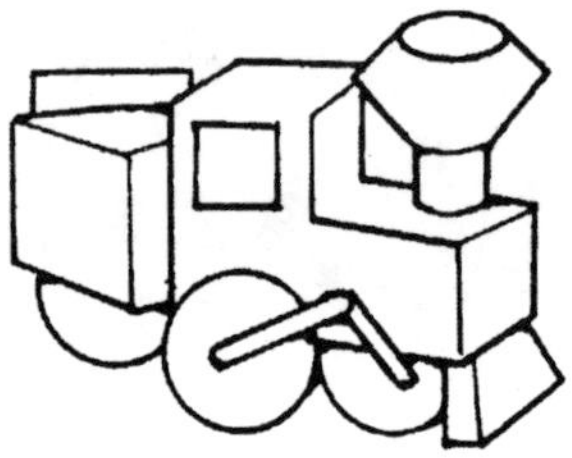

P ___   ___ q   ___ r

S ___   T ___   ___ u

V ___   W ___   X ___

___ y   Z ___

THE ALPHABET

Fill in the missing letters.

a	b	c	d	e
f	g	-----	-----	j
k	l	m	-----	o
p	-----	r	s	t
u	-----	w	x	-----
z				

Draw lines to match the words.

RAT	fan
FAN	sun
JUG	hen
SUN	rat
HEN	jug

ANT	key
CAT	boy
KEY	ant
BOY	net
NET	cat

OX

PIG

DOG

URN

MAN

man

urn

pig

ox

dog

toy

egg

van

lion

yak

YAK

LION

TOY

VAN

EGG